True Paranormal Hauntings

Bloodcurdling Stories Of Haunted Houses, People And Unknown Creatures: Unusual And True Paranormal Hauntings

Table of Contents

Like FREE books?

Would you like them delivered to you every week?

Do you like non-fiction books on a huge range of different topics?

We send out FREE e-books every week so we can share our books with the world!

We have FREE books every week on AMAZON that we send to our email list.

So if you want in, then visit the link at the end of this book to sign up and sit back and wait for new books to be sent straight to your inbox!

Introduction

As humans we have a fascination with the unknown. Our minds naturally drift towards finding out what we do not yet know. In the history of human civilization this desire to know the unknown has molded the thrust of progress. Our desire to explore the boundaries of our knowledge and experience have led to us setting foot on the moon, and on trying to figure out how the universe itself works, and how it all came about.

Religion, it seems, is antithetical to the spirit of knowing the unknown, but it really is. Religion is a manifestation of a desire to put a name to the unknown. Religion and science, thus are two directions towards the same desire we as humans have used to become the most advanced species on earth – the desire to figure out the unknown.

However, the desire to understand what has not been understood, to experience what has not been experienced and learn what is unknown, is most truly realized in us in our deep fascination with the paranormal. The word is a combination of the root words 'para' and 'normal', with the understanding that anything that is 'above', or beyond our conceptions of normality, is paranormal.

The word supernatural has also evolved from a similar context, coming from Latin and meaning 'above nature'. Paranormal is different from a hypothesis, which, while also beyond our understanding are nevertheless based on scientific observation. Paranormal, on the other hand, refers to a more instinctive and imaginative understanding of what cannot be explained.

This book aims to do something similar to the anecdotal approach of analyzing the paranormal. In keeping with the anecdotal approach, I do not intend to question the veracity of the following events mentioned in this book. Such a line of questioning ignores the purpose of the paranormal, its effects as well as the organic way in which the story about the supernatural grows to become a legend.

The paranormal is often derided as untrue or full of falsities, but in my opinion it is actually a keynote to human progress. As humans we have a fascination with the supernatural, which draws us to our primal instincts to keep surviving and progressing as a race.

Studying the paranormal as a narrative of humanity explaining the unknown to itself is a very interesting and fruitful way to studying our history. Further, even though like in all literature the supernatural events in different locations and areas are different, there is a common and universal theme that is true for all the studies and reports of the supernatural, and it is universal because all humans are connected by the same primal and instinctual feeling that has enabled our progress – fear.

I have already mentioned fear as something rooted in what we do not understand. The supernatural is thus what we fear – the unknown, in a safe space, which cannot and does not affect us directly...

Chapter 1:
Understanding The Paranormal

The paranormal is something that defies comprehension. Sometimes, things that cannot be explained are associated with the paranormal, and then when research techniques become sophisticated enough, the truth of the matter can be found. To give a relatively recent example, the tales of the legendary Bermuda Triangle gained interest from many.

None could explain why and how so many ships sank in a small location off the coast of Bermuda. They certainly could not explain how helicopters came to sink. In the absence of any reliable explanation of these events, the reason was often attributed to the supernatural and to the paranormal.

The legend of the Bermuda triangle has been variously attributed to UFO's, to lost items and metals from the mythical continent of Atlantis, and yes, a vengeful spirit as well. However, after the major research that has gone into disproving this myth, the current understanding has been that the many legends surrounding this place have been variously exaggerated, embellished, and found to be spurious.

To put this in a more historical and universal perspective, when man was first exposed to natural phenomena like natural disasters, lightning and thunder, and even the monsoon, there was no way to understand such events. Even the sun and the moon were unexplained entities.

This is the story of religion, actually, with the sun and the moon worshiped, as well as the monsoon. With the advent of farming, the monsoons became extremely important to the growth and progress of humanity, and in several areas the world over, it still is.

It is not surprising hence, that the foremost gods of many pantheons of religion have placed a God who operates in the sphere of rain above all, such as Zeus, the Greek God of thunderstorms, and the most powerful of the Gods, or Indra, the Indian God of lighting and rain, and the King of all Gods.

The paranormal, or the supernatural, are thus the first areas towards human progress. We always seek to learn what we do not yet know, and the supernatural tends to be the first step towards humanity explaining the things it doesn't yet know to itself. This is why research on paranormal behavior has attracted many people from all disciplines and interests.

The other reason it has is because it is genuinely fascinating, as it appeals both to our sense of scientific curiosity, as well as our imagination. It is as much a myth-making exercise as it is about solving them.

The paranormal is known to impact humans both negatively and positively. It is easy to say why the seemingly supernatural phenomena that affects us negatively are much more interesting to all. For one, they actually are closer to the root of what causes us to fear them.

Fear is an emotion deeply rooted in our primal need to understand. We do not fear specific things, but what we do not understand. Knowing something gives us the security to be able to use our ingenuity to try to solve a problem, but when we do not know the cause of a certain event, it becomes so much more difficult for us not to fear it, and to think rationally about it.

A combination of our deep fascination towards the unknown, and the instinctual and primal fear towards it has created some of the most engaging and imaginative exercises. Whether it be movies, books or poems, horror and the supernatural have dominated our thoughts and remains one of the genres with the most impact.

Since the supernatural is above our knowledge and beyond our ability to understand or to approach, the paranormal takes precedence over us. It is always viewed as more powerful, more accomplished and possessing qualities that we cannot possess. This is also why the analytical and scientific approach has so often taken a confrontational attitude towards those who believe in the supernatural.

Organized research on paranormal phenomena is very difficult. There are a lot of reasons for this, but the primary reason is that the paranormal, like a myth, grows organically to gain a life of its own. Embellishments, exaggerations and plain falsities are very common to literature about the supernatural. The work of the researcher thus becomes that much more difficult, as the researcher is forced to question the truth of each and every single piece of evidence.

The entire myth has to be deconstructed to figure out the truth of the matter. Further, by definition, the paranormal cannot be understood. If it is understood, it ceases to be the paranormal. Thus research in the field bucks the conventional.

Research is conducted on several basis's. One of them is the participant-observer approach (which by itself is not confined to paranormal studies.) The participant-observer approach essentially works on the principle that the more amount of time, energy and resources spent on research, the more qualitative data collected, the better, regardless of any actual insight.

Another is the skeptical scientific investigation approach. Here, claims of paranormal activity are rigorously investigated with the aim of applying the scientific method to figuring out the truth of the matter.

Skeptical scientific investigators believe that as far as the paranormal is concerned, it is not the event itself that creates the feeling of the paranormal but the feeling of fear and dread in the mind of the observer who ignores the completely rational solution to the problem and believes it is the supernatural.

This form of research, however, is often clouded, especially when you look at the past, because little physical evidence remains to be scientifically analyzed.

The anecdotal approach collects stories told by different witnesses about supposedly paranormal events. Usually the anecdotal approach does not itself analyze the event but leaves the responsibility of deciding if it is true or not to the reader. So without much ado, let us begin.

Chapter 2:
Princess Theater – Melbourne, Australia

The Princess Theater is one of Melbourne's landmarks and one of its oldest entertainment buildings. It is on the Victorian Heritage Register and is listed on the National Trust of Australia. It has also reportedly been haunted by the ghost of a dead actor for 127 years.

The Theater was first established in 1854, and included a central ring for horse racing and a stage at one end. It was renovated in 1886 with the world's first retractable ceiling, and featured state-of-the-art stage lighting. It opened to audiences with a performance of Gilbert and Sullivan's *The Mikado*.

The theater was hailed as being equal to some of the best theater halls in the world, including the Frankfurt Stadt, the Grand in Bordeaux and the Paris Opera. Several other renovations have since taken place, and the Princess Theater has solidified its reputation as one of the better theater halls in the world.

In 1888, after the staging of *The Mikado*, the Princess Theater began staging Gounod's opera, *Faust*. The old story of the devil tempting the ideal man and sending him to hell was very successful in its first run at the Theater. This is also when the Theater was introduced to its ghost.

Frederick Federici was a British opera singer who had gained much praise and fame for his work on the Savoy operas by Gilbert and Sullivan. He toured extensively from 1879 onwards, and played the lead role in the American production of *The Mikado*. He then toured Australia and acted the role of

Florian in the performance of *Princess Ida* at the Princess Theater, and then Harry Sherwood in Alfred Cellier's *Dorothy.*

He performed several of his old roles at the Theater as well, and earned some degree of fame. Many considered him as one of the most exciting and accomplished actors in the world. He then performed as part of Gounod's *Faust,* in the role of Mephistopheles, the role of the devil who attracted Faust and turned him to the side of Lucifer.

On the opening night, Federici was reported as having told his fellow actors that, "I will give a fine performance to-night, but it will kill me."

The performance did go well. In the climactic scene of the opera, the character of Mephistopheles drags Faust through the trapdoor under the stage to hell and they both leave the stage. It was at this time while the actors were being pulled through the trapdoor underneath that Federici, who had a history of heart disease suffered a heart attack and collapsed.

The audience and the other actors had no idea about what had happened as he was already in the trapdoor when this happened. He was taken to the Green Room immediately where a doctor present there tried to revive him but failed. He was only 37 years old.

The Press of Melbourne while writing about his tragic death reported "that he both sang and acted on Saturday night in a truly artistic manner and that he has never been seen to greater advantage than he was on that occasion." What had been some of his last words in his performance had come true.

The legend of his ghost also began on that very day. After the opera had finished, the directors called the actors and told them about what had happened underneath the stage during the final scenes of the opera. The actors were confused, and each and every one of them reported that they had seen Federici join the rest of them at the end of the play to take their bows.

Several members of the audience also mentioned that they had noticed him at the end of the play. From then on, the legend of his ghost has stuck and has forever been associated with the Princess Theater. Ghostly figures have been seen who have always been dressed exquisitely well amongst the front rows of the audience in the Theater.

He has also been spotted by audiences on the stage, and by the staff of the Theater in the make-up room, the corridors and even on the roof. A seat has been reserved at the Princess Theater for Federici on the third row of the dress circle ever since as a mark of respect.

Federici is also remembered in other ways, with the Federici bistro on the opposite end of the street named in his honor. Federici is one of the most famous ghosts in Australia, but he is also regarded as one of the friendliest. He has never displayed malicious intent and it is said that whenever he is sighted the days performance goes without a hitch and is well received.

However despite it being 127 years since his death, public interest in Federici has not dimmed. This is primarily because as recently as 1970, in a photograph of the famous actor Kennedy Miller for a documentary, one can clearly see a pale, translucent and well-dressed figure in the background. Both Miller and the photographer swear that they did not see, or feel, anything when the picture was taken.

The ghost represents Australia's, and especially Melbourne's interest in the paranormal in an interesting way. Like the other famous ghosts in Melbourne, such as the one in La Mama Theater and the cabaret venue The Butterfly Club, and the Lalor House in Richmond, these figures are usually European, well dressed and upper class.

They represent an intrusion of the past into the present, and much of Australia's past is dominated by discourse about the colonial era. Interestingly, ghosts have often been found at the theater halls, almost as if the paranormal has an association with the arts that cannot be reasoned out.

While Federici no longer reserves his usual seat in the third row of the dress circle of the audience any more, there has been an increase in sightings at the theater and the legend of the actor who died under the stage shows no sign of dimming for now.

Chapter 3:
Villa Dunardi – Sicily, Italy

Known amongst the locals as "La Villa dei demoni", or The Villa of the Demons, the Villa Dunardi is an uninhabited mansion near George Beach in Sicily, Italy. Built in 1964, the villa has been abandoned for as long as anyone remembers. In the 50 years or so since, the villa has been one of the most reported on sites for the paranormal in the entire world, with over 150 reported incidents of supernatural activity associated with it.

It is said that in its early years, the villa was reportedly the site for several séances. These communions with the dead were said to be tinged with demonic invocations. The villa was a mystery for the locals as well, as no one knew who had built the villa, or for whom it had been built.

The entire mansion was shrouded under a secret veil that none could pierce. It has always been vacant, yet no one had sold it, nor approached the owner to buy it. The locals did not know who owned the mansion, either.

The site remains a favorite place for "ghost-hunters" and those interested in the supernatural to explore. What is interesting is that the Villa is not a case of a single unexplained event, or two. The site has seen reports of varied paranormal phenomena of many different kinds.

Some of these include what the locals claim to be "courtesy", such as the opening and shutting of the doors, and the lights flickering. The top floor of the mansion apparently lights up at 3:20 AM for a few seconds.

Further, orbs of light have been seen around the house by explorers. Some claim a poltergeist has made the villa its abode. Another interesting oddity about the mansion is that while some claim the mysterious activity inside the villa are positively aimed towards the community, others claim the spirits inside are mischievous in nature.

Inside Italy, at least, the Villa Dunardi is known and spoken about by many. With more than 150 different sightings and a huge rate of reports about paranormal activity within the mansion, it was, according to the Italian Research Center CIR, rated as one of the 30 most haunted houses in the world in 2011.

The sheer number of the unexplained phenomena by all kinds of people, including locals who live nearby and report strange noises, shadows in absolute darkness and lights, as well as ghost hunters, who have gone further to report orbs of lights at specific times, apparitions, and visions lends an aura of mystery to the villa. While some have attempted a more rational break down of the villa's mysteries, none of them could explain how, without a working electrical connection, the lights at the villa are switched on when they enter.

What is also clear with respect to the villa is that it has remained a site of some gross exaggeration. Throughout the 50 years it has been around the villa has acquired a reputation that has been embellished by gross exaggeration and irrational fear. As of now, recent reports of the villa have included sightings of some strange luminous creatures that did not appear to be human.

In 1999 a couple who had been by the villa claimed that there had been a strange spaceship exactly overhead the villa at night. The reputation of the presence of a poltergeist was formed between 1982 and 1986. While some say this was actually because of some electrical fields that were around the villa as part of a construction activity, others claim that there was rogue research into electrical torture conducted by the government inside the villa, and that they encouraged stories of the supernatural to discourage people from entering the villa.

It does seem that the volume of different sightings suggests that most of the reports about the Villa Dunardi are false. However, yet again, the volume of sightings also suggests that there is a kernel of truth to the association of the villa with the paranormal. Whether there is a rational explanation to what has been happening in the villa is quite beside the point, it is the sheer number of different legends associated with the place that make the Villa Dunardi a point of interest to both tourists and locals.

Today the Villa Dunardi is the primary attraction of a resort of the same name. The resort includes tours of the house as part of its itinerary for visitors. The Villa Dunardi remains a site with some notoriety, with reports of strange lights and visions around the house coming in every few months.

Chapter 4:
The Dragsholm Slot Castle
– Zealand, Denmark

The Dragsholm Slot Castle in Denmark is a historical building built in the 12th century, which has influenced and shaped the events around it. The name Dragsholm actually is of Viking origin. In the Viking age, a drag meant a narrow stretch of land. Ships were dragged along this narrow stretch of land, to avoid dangerous and rocky waters.

The waters off the north of Zealand were especially prone to ships sinking. Dragsholm was built on an island just off the coast and literally means 'islet by the drag'. The castle was built by Peder Sunesen, the Bishop of Roskilde, who envisioned it as a residence for nobles and kings.

In the middle ages, it was a fortification during the several wars that took place in Europe at that time. During the Reformation period in Europe, Denmark was the site of a vicious war known as the Count's war. Dragsholm was the last castle opposing the Catholic armies of Count Christoffer who supported King Christian II.

Christian II was deposed and King Christian III became the new King of Denmark, and Dragsholm Castle moved to his care. Under Christian III, Dragsholm became a prison for high profile prisoners including nobles and ecclesiastical persons.

People imprisoned in this period included Joachim Ronnow, the former owner of the castle and the last proponent of Catholicism in the country. Ejler Brockenhus, popularly known as "The Mad Squire" was another. Perhaps the most high profile prisoner in Dragsholm was the third husband of

Mary, Queen of Scots, James Hepburn, the 4th Earl of Bothwell. More than 300 prisoners died in Dragsholm Castle, and it gained a fearsome and notorious reputation.

When Sweden invaded Zealand, the last inhabitants of the Castle attempted to blow it up, and the castle lay in ruins until King Christian V gave the castle over to a grocer, Heinrich Muller, to cover his debts. Muller began to restore the castle. The castle was sold in 1694 to noble Frederik Adeler who traced his ancestry to the Christian kings, and he remade it into a baroque castle.

The Adeler family made several changes to the castle in their time, owning the castle until they died in 1932, and the ownership of the Castle lapsed to the Central Land Board of Denmark. They sold it seven years later to the Bottger family. Today, the Dragsholm Castle includes two restaurants, a high profile conference room and a hotel. And over a hundred reported ghosts from amongst the prisoners that were imprisoned in the dungeons of the castle.

Joachim Ronnow died in the castle in 1544. He was imprisoned along with the other ecclesiastical prisoners in the north tower of the castle. While there have not been any sightings of his ghost specifically at the castle, there exist reports of wailing and Catholic chants from the same tower he was locked up in,.

The story of James Hepburn, on the other hand is far more substantiated. Captured in 1573, he was imprisoned in Dragsholm by King Frederik II. His captors gave him just enough food and water to survive, and tied him to a pillar and left him to die in a dungeon. It is said that Hepburn went mad and died in either 1578 or 1579.

The pillar to which he was chained can still be seen, with a circular groove on the floor where Hepburn supposedly had been chained. The Earl of Bothwell is one of the most frequent "visitors" to the castle. It is said that he rides into the courtyard riding on his horse or in his carriage, and many visitors have heard the sound of the hooves of a horse in the yard.

There are two prominent female ghosts that frequent the castle as well. One is referred to as the White Lady, and the other as the Grey Lady. While the origin stories of the female ghosts are unclear with multiple accounts, most claim the White Lady was a lady named Celina Bovles of the Bovles family. Celina reportedly fell in love with a commoner and consummated her love, becoming pregnant. When her father found out, he was furious and imprisoned her in the dungeons of the castle.

In the 1930's, workers renovating the castle found a skeleton of a woman dressed in white imprisoned in the dungeons of the castle, tied to a wall. This seems to be a corroboration of the historical accuracy of the legend of the White Lady.

However the linking of this skeleton with Celina Bovles, who is present in the prison logbooks has not been conclusively proven. In any case, the legend of the White Lady predates the discovery. The White Lady is said to move around the grounds of the castle, looking for her lost lover, and wailing in sorrow and dismay at her loss.

The Grey Lady is a more apocryphal story. It is said that she was a commoner of some uncommon beauty who worked at the castle. One day, she came to the castle with a debilitating toothache. The master of the castle prepared an herbal poultice for her, which cured her toothache. Shortly after this, the lady died of some unrelated incident.

However, her ghost haunts the castle to this day remaining in eternal gratitude towards the master of the castle for curing her toothache and looking to repay her debt. The Grey Lady is one of the beneficial reported ghosts, said to be a protector of the castle who watches over it. While sightings of the Grey Lady have been low as of late, hers is one of the enduring legends amongst the community around the castle.

Dragsholm Castle is a historical site of some significance, and it has both shaped and been shaped by the community around it. The haunted nature of the castle stems from it being a prison, notorious around Europe during the Reformation period. I

t was reported that the dungeons and towers of the castle were used as prisons, and that the prison was divided into zones depending on the nobility of the prisoner, the crime they had committed and their relationship with the King. Its historical significance to the community is a primary reason why the paranormal activity around it has been tinged by its long and colorful history.

Chapter 5:
The Ye Olde Man and
Scythe Pub – Bolton, UK

The Ye Olde Man and Scythe Pub is one of the oldest public houses in the United Kingdom, standing in Churchgate since the 12th Century. It is one of the best-known and most popular pubs in the Bolton town center today. The oldest mention of the pub in recorded history is in a Royal Charter signed in 1251 giving permission for a market to be held on the property by the Earl of Derby, who owned the property at the time.

Since then, the pub has undergone a few structural changes, being rebuilt in the 17th Century, though some parts of the building, especially the cellar dates back to the 12th Century in origin.

The name of the pub and its logo of the Scythe is also almost as old as the pub itself. The ownership of the property moved to the Pilkingtons through marriage a few years after the Royal Charter. The crest of the Pilkingtons is a man mowing a field with a scythe relating to a family legend of one of their ancestors who disguised himself as a mower to avoid being captured during the Norman Conquest.

At the Battle of Bosworth, the Pilkingtons fought for Richard the Third in 1485, and Leonard Pilkington was later executed at Leicester. All the property owned by the Pilkingtons was passed to the newly reinstated Earl of Derby, Thomas Stanley.

During the time of the Civil War, the Royalist sympathizer forces led by Prince Rupert stormed Bolton and killed more than 1500 people, including armed troops and civilians. Much of this slaughter took place in the town center, right outside the pub. However, the pub would soon see much more violence.

James Stanley was the 7th Earl of Derby. Previously Lord Strange before ascending to the Earldom, Stanley had not taken part in the Civil War because he hadn't been in the country. Once the fighting began, however, he sided with King Charles I.

Stanley was sent to fortify the Isle of Man by Charles I, and while away, his wife Charlotte de la Trenmoille and his family home, Lathom House came under siege by forces supporting the Parliament, led by Thomas Fairfax.

Stanley joined the forces of Prince Rupert and relieved the siege in 1644. This is said to be the event that led to the massacre at Bolton, and Rupert was now firmly turned against the Parliamentary cause. Following the war, Charles I was deposed and the Magna Carta was signed.

Stanley was arrested for treason, and executed in Bolton for his role in the infamous massacre. He was executed right outside the pub in the market place. Before his public execution he sat down for a last meal at the pub with the landlord, James Cockrel. The chair in which he sat dates from 1590 and is still displayed in the Museum Room of the pub.

Stanley was executed on October 15th 1651. Along with his chair, he is said to haunt the pub to this day. Ghostly specters have been seen seated in the pub. Security camera footage has also seen mysterious and translucent figures in the cellars of the pub. A beheaded man, whom many claim to be the ghost of Stanley is said to appear at certain points of time in the evening inside the hotel.

Other ghosts of a similar origin are also reported in the pub, with many tracing their history to the massacre of Bolton. A ghost in the form of a young female by the name of Jenny is often seen. It is believed that Jenny was imprisoned in the cellar of the pub by the Stanley family.

Séances conducted inside the pub have revealed that as many as a hundred and at least twenty-five ghosts inhabit the pub. Broken glasses have been found in the morning by the pub owners, with the security cameras having abruptly stopped working just after the event.

Similar to Dragsholm Slot, the Olde Man and the Scythe Pub, which is the oldest public house in Bolton and the fourth oldest in all the United Kingdom has a rich and illustrious history around it in its location at the town center in one of the United Kingdom's most important cities.

Even before the Bolton massacre and the subsequent execution of Stanley, the pub has been a witness to many events of much historical significance. The tales of the paranormal activity, like in Dragsholm Slot are colored by the many important events the pub has been witness to.

Chapter 6:
Zvikov Castle - Czech Republic

Zvikov Castle is known as the "King of Czech Castles" in the Czech Republic. It is located in the junction between the Vltava and Otava Rivers in the South Bohemian Region of the Czech Republic. Owing to the natural terrain surrounding the Castle it was always one of the most important regions strategically and tactically in the Czech Republic. The Castle as it is now known was built in the first half of the 13th Century on the orders of the King.

The exact details are unknown but the architecture of the Castle has been dated to that time. However, the Castle was actually built on the foundations of an old fort built here by the Celts anytime between the 2nd Century BC and the 1st Century AD. The area itself has been inhabited since prehistoric times.

The castle passed from different hands as Czechoslovakia passed through different hands, with every subsequent owner adding more fortifications to the Castle. The Castle acquired a reputation as the strongest in the Slavic regions after the Hussites besieged the fort for five months but were unable to take it.

In 1618, a group of 150 rebels held the Castle successfully against the troops of the Habsburg dynasty numbering 4000. These troops capitulated only after 4 years, and the castle was subsequently ransacked. A fire in 1750 further damaged the once renowned Castle, which was by now a site for farmers. The palace was in ruins until 1947 when renovations began and the site was modernized.

Supernatural stories about the Zvikov Castle have been around since the early 1500's. Stories of the Zvíkovský Rarášek, which is a common figure in Czech folklore, abound in the Castle. While there is no appropriate translation for the term in English, the closest term is the 'imp'.

Zvikov's 'imp' is said to be a mischievous but good-hearted figure. However, Zvikov's imp is not the only supernatural story around the Castle. Parts of the castle have remained from its early Celtish origins built in the 1st Century AD. They were built by the Marcomanni dynasty whilst ruling over Bohemia, which would become a part of the Zvikov Castle later.

The bricks at the foundations of the Castle have strange inscriptions on them, which have been a subject of mystery and linguistic interpretation for experts. This part of the Castle has been known for mysterious phenomena. It is said to be dangerous to sleep in the main tower of the Castle as none who have slept there have survived the next year.

In fact, while shooting a film about the Castle the crew slept in the main tower of the Castle as well, and they all ended up dead before the year ended. Those who have visited the Castle have reported that their electronic equipment and cameras have all experienced malfunctions, which are resolved only after they leave the castle.

The grounds of the castle are said to be populated by the legendary fire hounds of Czech myth. These fire hounds are said to guard over areas of importance and great treasure. The mysterious engravings on the bricks in the older part of the Castle also have received a lot of attention. Some claimed they had been left by extra-terrestrials, others by an old lost civilization and several other rumors.

However research based on the linguistic nature of these symbols came up with a much more rational yet not as sensational reason. The engravings on the bricks were found to have been left by the brick layers, who were known to leave a mark of their own making on every brick they made. This was found when another set of similarly marked bricks were found in the ruins of a fort a few miles away.

In its long history Zvikov Castle has earned a reputation of being haunted with a series of rumors and claims of the paranormal. Most of these rumors can be dated, and can be seen to have started at around the same time. Since the early 1500's the Castle has become one of the principal attractions to those interested in the paranormal.

Today, the restored Castle is open in the summer and spring months for tourists and hikers. Further, Zvikov's imp has been the subject of study both scientifically as well as artistically, serving as the inspiration for such works as Ladislav Stroupežnický's theatrical comedy Zvíkovský rarášek.

It remains one of the most notorious haunted areas in the world. Zvikov Castle has assimilated a series of stories from the supernatural. Many of the mysterious stories surrounding Zvikov Castle have yet to find a rational explanation. For example, electronic equipment still does not work properly in the castle, and no source for this problem has yet been found.

Chapter 7:
Vulcan Hotel – Otago, New Zealand

Known as the most haunted area in New Zealand, the Vulcan Hotel was originally called the Ballarat Hotel, and was built in 1832 from mud brick. It is in the town of Saint Bathans, and is the town's major tourist attraction. It is also present in the New Zealand Historic Places Trust.

It was restored and repaired during the 1850's and was renamed the Vulcan Hotel. The Vulcan Hotel is the only major haunted location in the entire country, and is thus of some significant importance to tourists and locals alike. A thoroughly normal hotel, the Vulcan Hotel was a small hotel in the town when a sensational case broke out in the 1880's.

A young woman had rented out room 101 for a while. After a few days, hotel staff found her raped and strangled to death in her room at the hotel. It was later found that she was actually a prostitute, with no information about her available except that she was called 'Rose' and that she had been entertaining clients in her room at the hotel.

Her murderer was never found. She had been the one renting the room, and none had seen anyone enter her room, or leaving it. The lack of DNA testing available at that point of time meant that her murderer would never be found that way.

Rose's ghost is said to haunt the Vulcan Hotel to this day. Despite the Vulcan Hotel's re-establishment after the controversy surrounding the event to become one of the most important tourist attractions in the country, the ghost of Rose continues to haunt the hotel. However she only haunts single men who stay the night in the hotel.

Reports from both members of the staff and guests at the hotel have reported seeing her lurking in the corridors of the hotel. She is usually to be found reclining on a chaise lounge in the formal dining room (which is left unoccupied as a mark of respect). However, while otherwise not showing any negative behavior, she does seem to have a vengeful spirit directed towards men. There have been multiple reports of men waking up to being strangled by an invisible spirit. They even have bruises and scratches to show for their escapades.

The hotel also witnesses other phenomena such as groaning to be heard in hallways. Staff report that kettles and pots with water or tea inside are found to be boiling despite the absence of any heating and doors, especially the room in which Rose was found murdered, 101, often lock and unlock of their own accord.

Guests can request to stay in the room she was found dead in. Her lounge in the dining room is also always left empty as a mark of respect to her. Recent attempts at investigating the recorded death of Rose have failed because of the lack of evidence to have survived from her case.

A seemingly transparent figure has also been caught hovering by security cameras. The sheer number of people to have reported a presence and the CCTV footage make the Vulcan Hotel one of the more convincing sites for the paranormal.

Chapter 8:
Alkimos – Perth, Australia

The Alkimos is the name of a Greek merchant ship, which, in 1963, hit rocks on the coast of Perth, in Western Australia and sank. The ship quickly became a famous and important tourist location, which led to the nearby town also naming itself after the ship.

The ship itself was built during World War II in Baltimore as part of the United States' 'Liberty Ship Program'. These ships were ones that were built extremely quickly to see action. In fact, the ship was said to have been built in just ten days. These ships were designed to be quick replacements to convoy troops quickly from one place to another, and to then be used as bait to draw out fire from the opposition.

It however saw just 9 days of active service for the United States, and was reassigned to a Norway based trading company, where it served for 18 months, primarily as a troopship transporting cargo and troops in convoys in the Mediterranean, often under heavy fire. The members of the ship, as was usual for troopships had members of all nationalities serving aboard.

In 1944 a Canadian radio operator was reported to have been shot by another member, who then shot himself. After the war it was sold to a Greek shipping company and renamed the Alkimos. It served as a merchant ship for 20 years. On its final voyage the ship struck some reefs off the west coast of Australia.

It was salvaged and managed to reach Perth, where it underwent repairs for two months. A dispute following the fees for the repairs saw the Alkimos leave, being towed by a ship heading for Hong Kong. Just a few hours after leaving Perth, the towline gave way, and the Alkimos was driven to the shore. A series of similar concerns and then a fire left the ship unsalvageable.

It was sold to a scrap company, as the ship remained on the coast. However all attempts to remove scrap from the ship were also abandoned after yet another fire broke out aboard and then sank the boat.

The ship had already developed a reputation for being cursed and jinxed, which only intensified after it sank. Rumors about the ship range from its workers having been sealed between the hulls during construction, a recurring complaint with Liberty Ships. Their ghosts are said to haunt the ship to this day.

A woman who was working on some repairs suffered a serious fall from the hull, and thus delivered a stillborn baby prematurely. This incident received a lot of press and the ships reputation as a jinxed ship was fixed in people's minds.

Later, salvage workers trying to get scrap from the ship reported several mysterious incidents such as tools being moved to different locations, noises and smells of something cooking emanating from the galleys, and footsteps near the ladder. The skull of a long distance swimmer was found in 1969 after he disappeared while attempting a swim between Rottnest Island and Cottesloe Beach.

Researchers who have worked on finding out more about the ship have also had several problems. A US Navy submariner who had assessed the wreck died in a plane crash. Researcher Jack Wong Sue, who researched the ship intimately and even wrote a book containing all the many legends associated with the ship got a severe but unidentified respiratory disease. It is also claimed that horses being ridden nearby refuse to enter the area near where the ship is wrecked.

A ghost popularly named Henry is also said to walk upon the ship wearing rubber shoes and roams around on the deck of the ship. Henry has reportedly even conversed with some people. This apparition has been witnessed by fishermen, salvage workers and divers.

The specter of ill-luck hangs very prominently about the ship. From the time of its construction it has reported several cases of ill-luck for the people around it. During its service in the Mediterranean Sea it was once left completely unguarded on top of a reef after two ships in front of it were bombed, before it reached high tide and the ship could continue its journey.

In total, after being wrecked, the ship was bought by 9 different salvage companies, all of which were unable to salvage the metal on the ship as a series of misfortunes including the aforementioned incident of the woman who suffered a nasty fall, several fires, and trouble with machines led to each effort being stopped in its tracks.

All owners of the salvage companies suffered serious financial misfortune after buying the ship, ranging from bankruptcy to severe illness, and in the case of two of the owners, death. In fact, even during its construction there were several mishaps that occurred, and the main builder of the ship was found dead a few months after he completed building it.

Jack Wong Sue was not supposed to survive after his medical illness, but after ten months he managed to recover, and completed the book he had been writing, named the *Ghosts of the Alkimos,* which remains one of the most comprehensive analyses of the several paranormal incidents related to the ship.

Today the remains of the ship can be found a short drive off the coast of Perth, and is a popular location for divers. However it is very dangerous because portions of the wreck have been known to collapse without warning.

It doesn't matter if it is really a haunted ship or a series of unfortunate coincidences; *Alkimos* has acquired a reputation as unlucky and jinxed, which cannot be denied. The series of questionable incidences of bad luck across continents and hemispheres that have followed this ship have been more of a hint that anything else.

One of the most interesting, scary facts about the ship is that horses do not approach the beach near to which the ship has sunk, and dogs also do not approve of the area. It has become one of history's most enduring legends associated with the paranormal and supernatural.

Chapter 9:
Chase Vault – Christ Church, Barbados

The Chase Vault was a family burial vault located in the cemetery of the Christ Church Parish Church in Oistins. The vault gained international renown after a series of mysterious events were reported around the vault.

In 1833, a research document was published claiming that a Mrs. Goddard was buried in the vault in 1807, followed by the burial of Ann Marie Chase in 1808, and then Dorcas Chase in 1812. The report claimed that when the vault was opened again in late 1812 to bury Thomas Chase, the positions of the coffins of the two Chase girls had been interchanged, and the whole vault was in a state of disarray quite unlike what it had been when it was closed.

When the vault was opened again to bury another infant, all four of the coffins inside were reorganized again and had been disturbed. The mysterious part of the story was that all the coffins were made of lead and were extremely heavy.

In fact, the deaths themselves were a little mysterious. The Chase family headed by Thomas Chase was not well liked by the locals because of their poor treatment of their slaves. Dorcas Chase died under mysterious circumstances. It was said that she was dissatisfied with her family's cruel treatment of slaves.

When she protested, she too was treated cruelly by her father. Thus she committed suicide by starving herself. A month later, when Thomas Chase died, the official report said that his death, too, had been by suicide.

Each time the vault was opened the coffins inside it were rearranged (it took four men at the very least to lift a coffin) and then the vault door was shut. The vault door is made of stone and took at least seven to eight men at the same time to lift it. Though the floor was sand, there were neither any marks nor footsteps. Yet the places of the coffins were regularly interchanged.

The vault was built by a James Elliot in 1724. It was designed with carved stone and coral and with concrete walls, which were over two feet thick. An enormous blue slab of marble guarded the vault. It was purchased by the Chase family in 1808, when Mrs. Goddard was the only person to be buried inside, and chose to keep her body in the vault.

The infant Ann Marie Chase was the first one from the family to be buried there. It is said that James Elliot's wife, Elizabeth had also been buried in the vault, but when Mrs. Goddard was buried there was no other coffin found.

At first, the members of the family thought that this was the work of grave robbers. However there was nothing of value at the vault that had been stolen and the amount of effort needed to open the vault and then move the heavy coffins seemed to have no explanation. In 1816, the vault was opened to bury the body of a young boy.

The coffins were once again disturbed, including the 240-pound lead coffin of Thomas Chase. Just two months later another person died and was to be buried in the vault. By now the vault had gained something of a reputation and was thoroughly checked from the outside. However all the coffins were yet again displaced despite the vault being airtight as well as the stone door not being touched.

Mrs. Goddard's coffin was not displaced, but had been heavily damaged by another coffin, such that her body was actually peeking out of the coffin. A detailed investigation was called for. The vault was cleaned, marked with the seal of the Governor and sprinkled with sand.

A detailed drawing was made and the vault was kept under surveillance from the outside for the next two years, before it was opened again. Though no activity had seemed to happen from the outside, the coffins inside had been moved violently again, with the baby Ann Marie Chase's coffin being chipped and leaning against the door of the vault.

This incident led to the Chase Vault becoming an international phenomenon. Several people provided different reasons, rational and otherwise for the mystery. *Sherlock Holmes'* writer Arthur Conan Doyle, a committed believer in the supernatural advanced that it was the restless spirit of the two members of the vault who had committed suicide, Dorcas Chase and Thomas Chase that had disturbed the other coffins.

The most telling piece of evidence for this claim was that the coffin had only seen changes after Dorcas had been buried. Other claims included that Mrs. Goddard was actually a vampire who had been imprisoned there to make sure she wouldn't get out.

Rational explanations over the years have included earthquakes, which certainly could have moved the coffins, but this explanation was rejected because the other vaults in the cemetery would have been affected as well. Human tampering was also rejected because of the difficulty of getting into the vault in the first place, leaving aside lifting up coffins heavier than most men.

Further, to have a coffin leaning against the door would have made it impossible for humans to leave the vault. Another popular theory had been flooding, as flooding would have made it possible for the coffins in the vault to move. However, the sand that had been sprinkled on the floor before shutting it had been undisturbed, making that theory weak as well.

The Chase family removed all the bodies from the vault and buried them in another cemetery, and no other body would be buried in Chase Vault again. It remains empty to this day, unopened for nearly two centuries. The mystery remains unsolved.

Other skeptical investigators have claimed that the Chase Vault stories are in fact a Masonic allegory, but also add that the historical documents about the vault are dubious. One of the major Masonic stories surrounds a secret vault that was symbolic of death, and where the truth of death can be found.

Thomas Chase and Samuel Brewster, the last person to have been buried in the vault were said to be members of Ancient Free and Accepted Masons. Skeptical investigators on this line of thought have noted several symbols, words and leitmotifs in the stories surrounding the vault and the vault itself that would be of interest to a Freemason. Skeptics conclude that the story is an elaborate Masonic allegory that traces back to another vault with a similar story, except that this one happened in 1844.

Further, the originality of the stories has been disputed. The first written reports of the story emerge in 1833, and do not credit a source. Official church records record the burials, but not the mysterious goings-on reported by these tales. In 1907 Andrew Lang provided the most thorough research on the Chase Vault yet, uncovering not only church records but the comments that were said to have been made by the Governor himself.

Lang also uncovered several second hand accounts of the tales, all of which seemed to have been anecdotes written by the parish of the Church, Thomas Orderson. Nearly every legend about the vault, which has survived today, is an exaggeration or an extension of one of Orderson's stories.

In general, Chase Vault is considered an elaborate hoax, because of a lack of first hand and sourced evidence about the vault. It is said that the legend around the vault became popular only in 1833 and onwards. However, it is also true that there indeed was a mystery around the vault, and that no rational solution could be provided.

The vault remains empty to this day, but it is clear it was completely airtight and that there were no tunnels or other entries. Perhaps there was something supernatural about the location after all.

Chapter 10:
Tambun Inn – Ipoh, Malaysia

The Tambun Inn is a somewhat famous hotel with a seedy reputation in Ipoh, Malaysia. It is said to be one of the most haunted locations in Malaysia. It lies next to a Chinese cemetery, which is one of the premier locations for the involvement of Ghosts according to the stories that surround the place.

Tambun Inn was at least around in the 50's, though no conclusive dates for the construction of the building have been found. It was originally known as the King's Hotel, and was owned by Lee Kwee Foh's family. It was later acquired by a mining tycoon and was renamed the Tambun Inn.

It was initially popular for inviting young musicians to perform at the hotel, and the performances at the inn quickly became popular amongst the younger people of Ipoh. This was also the time the ghost stories began about the Inn.

For starters, there is a legend surrounding the road to the Inn itself, called the Tambun Road. It is said that near the gates of a cemetery an old lady dressed in red tries to hail unsuspecting passersby. While no one knows what this figure aims to do, the superstitious people of Ipoh generally do not stop to get passengers at night in the location, and there are several (mostly apocryphal) tales of this lady being a ghost who attacks unsuspecting taxi drivers while in the backseat.

The hotel itself has gained a similar reputation. There have been multiple experiences of unexplained events from both staff and guests. Guests have claimed strange flickering lights in the dead of the night. The ghost of an elderly lady from the cemetery nearby reportedly haunts the roof of the hotel.

Guests have reported that they have heard whispers and screams in the dead of night. Lights turn on and off as well. Other guests have reported having heard the sound of children in the corridors at night playing and rushing about, followed by a woman screaming at them in Malay.

However in the morning it was revealed that the entire floor was empty and that no one, especially no children checked into the hotel at night. This has been reported several times by different people.

Further, other guests report having woken up in different locations with strange bruises on their bodies. One guest claimed to have been woken up by a young girl bouncing a ball on the wall of his room in the dead of night. The girl was dressed in a blue dress and appeared to be completely normal, but did not respond to the person. She stopped bouncing her ball and left, and the next morning the guest found out that no person of such a description had entered the inn. CCTV footage however backed up his experience of talking with the young girl.

Tambun Inn is not exactly a tourist spot but is well known amongst the locals for being in a strange and scary location. The area is also said to be the site of a mass-torture carried out by soldiers before the end of World War II. The large cemetery nearby has been vacant and not been used for a while, adding to the hint of mystery surrounding the place.

There have been many unexplained phenomena around the hotel, and the very persisting idea of the lady dressed in red. Further, an elderly lady has also been seen hovering around the hotel, as well as being seen on its roof. Despite the whispers of ghost activity, the lack of any serious involvement around the hotel make the Tambun Inn a valued location around Ipoh, and a favorite for ghost hunters as well as skeptics to check the place out.

Skeptics have claimed that the ghost stories around the hotel are part of a publicity stunt to promote the inn, but historically speaking the ghost stories around the area actually predate the construction of the hotel itself, with written records dating back to the late 19th century claiming there to be a ghost of an elderly lady haunting the junction the hotel is currently on.

In any case, several of the guests have reported mysterious apparitions and incidents that have not been explained. CCTV evidence further indicates the presence of something out of the ordinary in the location. The community around the Tambun Inn have developed several more stories around the spirits said to reside inside or around the Tambun Inn, which have become common folklore around the area. The Tambun Inn is one of Malaysia's most well known haunted locations, but it is also one of the world's enduring mysteries.

Chapter 11:
Koh-i-Chiltan - Quetta, Baluchistan

Koh-i-Chiltan is the name of the summit of a mountain in the Chiltan mountain group of the Sulaiman Mountain Range in Western Pakistan. It is the summit of a steep and rocky mountain known as Chiltan or Chehel Tan, which translates to "Forty bodies". It is the highest peak in the Chiltan mountain group at 10,500 feet. It is located in the capital of the province of Baluchistan, Quetta, and is the third highest mountain in Quetta, and the fifth highest in Baluchistan overall.

The mountain is said to be haunted, and the local community around the mountain regard it with both fear and devotion. It is said that a couple lived near the mountain and were trying to have a child, but were not successful. Desperate, they went to a holy man asking him for advice and to ask Allah to pray for a child on their behalf. The holy man told them that he could not change the will of God and give them a child.

On the other hand, the holy man's son, who was also a mendicant who was famous across the land, was confident he could grant their wish. He placed 40 pebbles he had found from the mountain on the lap of the woman and performed a ritual. Subsequently, each of the pebbles became children.

The couple was still not pleased by their fate, as they knew it was impossible for them to raise forty children. They decided on a strategy. The next day the father abandoned thirty-nine of the children on the Koh-i-Chiltan and decided to keep just the one with them.

However after a few years the mother, who had been harboring feelings of remorse and guilt decided to journey to the top of the mountain peak so that she could gather her no doubt dead children's remains. However when she reached the top of the mountain she was astounded that all the children were alive.

Praising Allah, she climbed back down the mountain to search for her husband to tell him the surprising and happy news. However she was unable to find him. Thus she decided to take the one child the couple had kept to the mountaintop so that the child could meet its siblings.

However when she reached the peak none of her children could be found. The woman decided to sleep on the peak of the mountain for a night with her child to lure her other children again. However, when she woke up the next morning, the children were not around, and the child she had kept, the fortieth child had also disappeared.

This incident gave the Balochi name of "Forty bodies" to its peak. Around the mountain it is said that the wails of the children can still be heard on the wind. While earlier people would climb the peak of the mountain, people were banned from climbing it after several reported that they would undergo some misfortune while climbing the relatively short, but steep mountain.

The mountain almost surrounds Quetta, and is also referred to as Koh-e-murdar, or the Mountain of the Dead. Only two Europeans have ever succeeded in climbing the mountain, Sir Henry Green and another man known only as Massan. The ascent is tough, and none of the natives ever help anyone in climbing the mountain.

The mountain is thus of some significance in Baluchistan, and is one of the most significant haunted locations in Pakistan.

However, the haunted mountain is different from others because the origins of the story that many attribute to its haunted nature does not come from a historical or apocryphal source, but one that is mythical. This means that it is difficult, impossible and unnecessary to try to date the event, or to try and find a rational explanation.

For example, the holy man's son gives the couple forty pebbles, which turn into children. However the truth of the matter is that the beliefs of the locals have constructed the myth. The haunted nature is not reflected in any religious titles (while some are devoted to the mountain, the true extent of that devotion is a small shrine on the peak of the mountain where the father reportedly left the children.

The mountain is feared but is also seen by the people of Quetta as a protector, due mostly to its unique shape wherein it seems to be covering the capital city of the province. The question with respect to Koh-i-Chiltan, thus, is whether the myth came first or if the haunted nature of the peak was first cast in light.

It is likely that the natives of Baluchistan, who have lived in the area for centuries with little to no exposure to the outside world, have remained in that area since then. This story came to light in an anecdote told in a book called *A ride to India across Persia and Baluchistan* by Harry De Windt, who was a travel writer of some renown that was a pre-1923 written work. There is every indication that this is a myth that has been constructed over time.

Both the Europeans who managed to climb the mountain admitted that the sound they heard while on the peak sounded like many children were wailing at once. The mountain can only be described as a sight for sore eyes, with a beautiful and sublime view of the entire province. The addition of a story which cannot be verified and which cannot be dated because of its origin in spoken legends passed down from generations makes the Koh-i-Chiltan, and it's 40 ghost children one of the enduring legends of today.

Chapter 12:
Kamchanod Forest – Udon Thani, Thailand

Kamchanod Forest is a small forest located on an island cut off by small canals from the village of Wang Tong in the Udon Thani district of Thailand. Kamchanod Forest is of great importance to the mythologically inclined in Thailand. It is said to contain the entrance to the lair of the legendary Phaya Naga. The Phaya Naga is a great snake that is worshiped in both Thailand and Laos, and are said to be the origins of the 'Naga Fireballs'.

The Naga Fireballs are said to be glowing lights that hover around the River Mekong, which seem to rise from the water very quickly to heights of up to two hundred meters, with observations ranging from a few hundred to many thousands of such fireballs being seen in a night. The fireballs themselves have undergone a lot of research around them, to try to figure out a rational cause for such fireballs to naturally occur.

Though some have reported that the fireballs are actually cannon shots by soldiers, the sheer volume of them seems to disregard that case from being true. Other natural causes such as chemical reactions in the marshes at the edge of the river have also been disproved. Plasma physics has also been used to try to advance a reason for these fireballs.

Kamchanod Forest is said to be the entrance to the lair of this protective figure that is worshiped in both Thailand and Laos as a protective figure for the respective tribes. The fireballs shot by the Naga culminate in the Fireball festival where tens of thousands of people gather at the banks of the River Mekong to watch the fireballs emerge.

The forest thus contains a shrine and several other sites of importance to those who believe and worship in the Phaya Naga. However, in 1987, something happened in the forest that would go on to become the site of one of Thailand's biggest unsolved mysteries and one of the most enduring paranormal stories in the world.

In 1987, a telephone call from a stranger to a mobile cinema projection company requested them to come for a night of entertainment at a specified location in the forest. The person who made the call refused to give any identifying details whatsoever, and wired the fees to the company. Therefore, though this request was strange, the company accordingly sent a team of four workers to the specified location.

In any case such nights of entertainment were not entirely unheard of. The crew assumed that the audience would be the villagers of the nearby village of Wang Tong. They reached the location early in the evening and began setting up the screen, and picking the films.

However, no one had arrived to watch the films by 9 PM, which was the time when the caller had said the entertainment should begin. In keeping with the caller's wishes, the crew began rolling the films to an empty venue.

As the night went on, however, a large group of villagers assembled slowly in front of the screen. They seemed to be commoners dressed in black and white. The crew noticed that several members of this audience looked strange, but did not pay much attention. The women were all dressed in white and sat on the right hand side, while the men were all dressed in black and sat on the left hand side.

This audience sat and watched the films throughout the night, and did not utter a single word throughout. They showed neither any emotion nor expression throughout the entire experience. At 4 in the morning all the films had been watched, and the crew packed up their equipment and headed to the village of Wang Tong.

In Wang Tong, they asked around about the strange crowd who had not spoken a word or uttered a cry while watching movies throughout the night, and were shocked to hear that no person in the entire village had even known they were screening movies. Though the village was quite close to the forest and to the location, they also had not heard the sound of the loudspeakers the crew had set up either.

It was only then that the crew began to realize that they must have been showing movies throughout the night to an audience of ghosts. The villagers returned to the forest with one member of the crew to try to find them, but no one could be found. Attempts to trace the number that had called the company also failed.

Kamchanod Forest, already a very sacred and renowned location in Thailand because of its reputation as the entrance to the lair of the Naga became the site of much more research, however the audience of hundreds of people had simply disappeared. Footprints could be found at the open-air location the films had been screened in, but they too had led to nowhere. The mystery has remained unsolved to this day, and has become a part of popular folklore in all of Thailand.

Recently, a film about the experience was released. The film, named The Screen at Kamchanod is a Thai film released exclusively on Netflix, and details a crew that tries to recreate the same experience. They succeed, but this time the ghosts are vengeful and the crew gradually lose their sanity. The film despite not garnering much critical acclaim did pretty well in terms of viewership.

Thus Kamchanod Forest is just a series of questions. Who was the caller? Who was this mysterious audience? Where did they come from, and more importantly, where did they disappear to? Why were they interested in watching films? None of these questions have been answered. The sheer absurdity of the situation has lent an increased aura of mystery to the events.

It remains an unsolved mystery, which, with the audience of ghosts has become a sensational story. We may never know what really happened that night, but the forest has already become something of a tourist attraction in the years since.

It also has excited the curiosity as well as the fear of some of Thailand's most prominent investigators. The absurd nature of the event and its aftermath have definitely placed what transpired at Kamchanod as a place where no explanation seems to fit except for the paranormal.

Chapter 13:
Jeruk Purut Cemetery, Jakarta, Indonesia

Jeruk Purut is a cemetery that covers a region of 9 hectares in Jakarta. It is one of the largest and most well-maintained cemeteries in Indonesia. In 2007, land donated was added to the cemetery. It is one of the busiest cemeteries in Jakarta, with an average of 300 burials per month.

The cemetery has been around for an unknown period of time, but was renovated and remodeled in the late 1950's to its current form. The cemetery is also the site of one of Indonesia's enduring ghost stories. In 2011 it was voted as the scariest place in Indonesia.

The site itself is undoubtedly scary. There are few lights available at night, and the presence of forests nearby give rise to several sounds in the dead of night, like howls and roars. Further it is easy to slip and fall on the cobbled path of the cemetery.

Jeruk Purut is said to harbor a specific ghost, however. The ghost of a pastor, who was decapitated and is thus headless is said to move around the cemetery during the nighttime. The ghost seemingly isn't intentionally malicious, but there have been several reports of the ghost not welcoming entry into the cemetery.

There are several rumors as to why the pastor is headless. One of them is that the ghost in a pastor's dress is not really a pastor but someone who tried to impersonate the pastor after killing the original pastor to hide from some crime. However, the villagers found out about it and had him beheaded publicly. Other rumors include that the pastor was out hunting when he was caught by some bandits and they beheaded him.

In any case, the ghost of the headless pastor is an enduring legend around the cemetery and the area. Though no dates have been found, and no historical source has been produced, a lot of anecdotal evidence has been found that corroborates the story of a pastor being beheaded.

However another thing most anecdotes about this event agree upon is that the pastor was not actually buried in Jeruk Purut, but in the nearby Tanah Kusir cemetery. In this context, why the ghost of a pastor chose to haunt a cemetery they were not even buried in is a mystery.

The pastor is often seen wandering in the company of the ghostly specter of a large, black dog. It is reported by those who have observed this ghost that the ghost, though headless, carries its decapitated head in its hands. He is said to visit certain graves. There are a plethora of local myths about this ghost, with some claiming that an odd number of people visiting the cemetery on Friday night can see and even talk with the ghost.

Hantu Jeruk Purut (The Ghost of Jeruk Purut) is one of the enduring ghost stories in Indonesia. It dates its origins to at least the 19th Century and perhaps even beyond. In 2006 a film was made that was inspired by the mystery surrounding the cemetery, named *Hantu Jeruk Purut*. The film did extraordinarily well in Indonesia, further increasing the popularity of the cemetery.

There are several interesting incidents that happened during the shooting of the film. For instance, before the film started the entire crew traveled to the cemetery and asked for the ghost's permission to shoot the film. Almost as if in response, two people present, an actress and a reporter fainted.

The local religious expert diagnosed that they had been possessed. The crew attempted to communicate with the spirit, but received no response. They offered various gifts to the spirit in glass containers, including cigars, chicken eggs, coffee and sugar before beginning to shoot the film.

The chain of mysterious events did not end. Several unexplained events happened during filming of the movie, which was shot primarily in surrounding areas to the cemetery such as abandoned houses and hospitals. Some of the crew reported seeing the spirit of a child suddenly appear while filming an important scene.

Further, while filming a climactic scene in which some scissors are used to attempt a stabbing, the actress lost control of the scissors, and they hit the temple of another actress, sending her to hospital.

The tales surrounding Jeruk Purut also has its naysayers, who claim that it is a myth that is perpetuated by some people. However, there appears to actually be no reason to do so, as unlike the nearby 'Potato Museum', which is also said to be haunted, there appears to be no financial incentive to do so. Further, the story at Jeruk Purut by far predates the movie, which was made at a time when most in Indonesia were at least aware of the stories surrounding the site.

Today Jeruk Purut is one of the most well-known haunted regions in Indonesia. It has been the subject of national attention and is one of the more popular tourist spots in Jakarta as well. While the authenticity of these events can and should be debated, as well as the existence of the ghost itself, the story has become popular culture to the local citizens of the country as well as tourists, and the area has become one of the most well known haunted locations in the world.

Conclusion

Why does the paranormal exist? What is its function in a society, especially in a highly modernized, skeptical and well informed society such as ours? Many have sought to disregard the existence of the paranormal entirely. Perhaps they are right, and the paranormal really does not exist. However, that does not mean the paranormal is not important. We tend to believe in the paranormal because it fulfills a certain need of our psyche.

Psychologically speaking, the major difference between the scientific method and paranormal investigation is belief. When we talk about the supernatural we have to incorporate a suspension of disbelief, as the supernatural is by definition something that is outside the scope of our knowledge.

Science, on the other hand, presents evidence to provide proof for an argument, and therefore it aims to stretch the boundaries of available knowledge, but the supernatural exists outside of the sphere of knowledge as a whole. When we talk of the paranormal, we are not talking about something that cannot be explained, but something whose explanation lies outside the current knowledge we have.

It doesn't seek to expand on the available knowledge, but to present a solution outside of it.

Believers in the supernatural will always believe in it, because no matter how hard we try we cannot know everything. Since we cannot know everything, the paranormal becomes a new way of understanding knowledge, which exists outside knowing something, or not knowing something.

Remember, the paranormal does not explain what we do not know, but rather exists outside the boundaries of knowledge itself. We cannot know the paranormal; because once we do know it, it will cease to be the paranormal. The belief in the paranormal is thus a different way of looking at the idea of knowledge.

While it seems to be at odds with the scientific method, it doesn't have to be. Since the supernatural exists outside the boundaries of available knowledge, it can be believed in whilst using the scientific approach.

In the tales of haunted houses, mansions and unsolved mysteries, a common thread can be seen, and that is how the story comes about. For example, the peak in Baluchistan and the story of the Naga Fireballs seem to have little in common, but they are both myth making exercises which are created by the experience of something tangible. I

n the case of the former, it is the sound of the high pitched wailing near the mountain peak, and in case of the latter, it is the emergence of strange lights from a future. Both of these fall outside the sphere of our knowledge, and then evolve over time to become a myth. A myth is a collection of stories, beliefs and attitudes that are lent weight and authenticity by any proof or evidence but the passing of many periods of time.

Dragsholm Slot and the Ye Olde Man & Scythe Pubs are historical buildings that are part of a community around it. Both of these 12th century buildings were witness to important historical events that shaped the progress of the community. Thus it is almost obvious that the stories and legends associated with these places are subject and witness to the same rich history the buildings themselves are steeped in.

The stories of the paranormal associated with these buildings are as influenced by the history of the building as the community itself is, and the story grows organically with the community to become the legend.

The Princess Theater and the Vulcan Hotel were both relatively normal establishments, until a specific tragic and horrific event occurred. In the former an actor died during a performance, and in the latter a young prostitute was found murdered in her bed in the morning and the killer was never found.

Here, the story of the paranormal is thus built on the tragedy itself, rather than the history of the building or of the ghost. These events, which shake up the community around the building, thus become the products of the ghost story.

In my opinion, the paranormal is pretty similar to the production and consumption of art. While it seems that there is an aesthetic sense to be appreciated in art, the truth of the matter is that all art is a reflection of our society. The history of the art that has been consumed can be used to make a history of the way society has changed.

I am interested in the paranormal in a similar manner. It is not the ghosts or spirits themselves that interest me, but the narratives that are drawn from a mysterious circumstance. Some of these are genuinely unsolved mysteries, such as the moving coffins in the Chase Vault or the ghosts who wanted to see a movie in Kamchanod forest. Other seem to have an obvious solution, and in other cases the sheer volume of reported incidents pushes them to become an area of concern.

What is common to all of these disparate tales of mystery, horror and the unknown from all parts of the world, however, is not the existence of the paranormal itself, but the way the narratives of the supernatural have been formed. Studying the shifts in how we approach the narrative of the paranormal, like studying the changes in our appreciation of art, can be a suitable study of ourselves.

The paranormal thus becomes less of the event or building in question, and more about ourselves. This is why analytical approaches to paranormal investigations fail, because they fail to take into account the subjectivity of views. An objective study of a supernatural event cannot be made, because the supernatural works differently for every person.

A system of analyses to find an objective truth, such as the analytical and rational approach fail not because of something intrinsically wrong with the approach, but an incompatibility with the subject that is being studied.

The paranormal defies knowledge. It is not known, or unknown, but something that exists outside of this realm. Thus when the analytical approach attempts to know what cannot be known, it is defeated. It may succeed in deconstructing the paranormal, but then it fails to be a study of it, because the supernatural cannot be known.

Any study of the paranormal thus ought to respect this nature of it. It ought to respect the boundary that the paranormal creates between the spheres of our available knowledge and our experience, and strive to maintain it. For this, a suspension of disbelief is often needed.

In this respect, the paranormal is similar to art as an exercise of imagination. This is why I believe that an anecdotal form of studying the paranormal is more effective. It allows for a multiplicity in views, and for a more varied understanding of the theme.

The paranormal works on our psyche through the primal instinct that centuries of evolution have only intensified in humans – fear. Fear remains the dominant feeling that controls what we do, the people we talk to, and what we desire. In today's age of scientific inquiry, what humanity fears above all is the unknown.

This is not a processed fear but something that is much more instinctive in nature. Our primal instincts still take root in some of the most common phobias exhibited by most - we fear the dark because in the dark we cannot see and thus cannot know, what is happening; we fear heights because we fear the sensation of falling and the helplessness associated with it; we fear death because we do not understand it at all; and many more.

The reason fear affects us so much, however, is because we are attracted to the very thing we fear. This is why we watch horror movies, because they offer us a safe space wherein what we fear and what we desire can be consumed at once, and this is why we are so fascinated by and so deeply affected by, as a community, in the supernatural.

The supernatural is a space where what we fear – the unknown can co-exist with what we do know, without contradicting or nullifying it. We are so deeply affected by the supernatural because it provides us the security of not knowing.

On that note, I would like to thank you yet again for choosing to purchase this book. As an act of imagination and creativity, it can be argued that there is nothing more fun and engaging than the paranormal. I hope that the unknown and misunderstood stories as mentioned in this book guide you to question what you do know and what you do understand, because that is what the paranormal is all about – questioning the boundaries of our knowledge and knowing that it will forever be incomplete.

Also, if you liked this book I would love it if you could leave me a review on Amazon! Just search for this title and my name on Amazon to find it. Thank you so much!

Other Books Written By Me

Below you'll find some of my other popular books that are popular on Amazon and Kindle as well. You can visit my author page on Amazon to see other work done by me. (Joseph A. Mudder).

True Crime Stories

True Paranormal Hauntings

True Paranormal Hauntings – Book 2

You can simply search for these titles on the Amazon website with my name to find them.

LIBRARY BUGS BOOKS

Like FREE books?

Would you like them delivered to you every week?

Do you like non-fiction books on a huge range of different topics?

We send out FREE e-books every week so we can share our books with the world!

We have FREE books every week on AMAZON that we send to our email list. If you want in, then visit the link below to sign up and sit back and wait for new books to be sent straight to your inbox!

It couldn't be simpler!

www.LibraryBugs.com

If you want FREE books delivered straight to your inbox, then visit the link above and soon you'll be receiving a great list of FREE e-books every week!

Enjoy :)

CPSIA information can be obtained
at www.ICGtesting.com
Printed in the USA
LVHW030957110720
660407LV00003B/869